# juices
### and tonics

# juices
## and tonics

elsa petersen-schepelern

photography by william lingwood

RYLAND
PETERS
& SMALL

LONDON NEW YORK

**Senior Designer**  Louise Leffler
**Food Stylist**  Elsa Petersen-Schepelern
**Editor**  Maddalena Bastianelli
**Production**  Patricia Harrington
**Photographer's Assistant**  Carl Davis
**Art Director**  Gabriella Le Grazie
**Publishing Director**  Anne Ryland

## Acknowledgements

My thanks to my sister Kirsten, to Louise Leffler for her mouthwatering
design and to William Lingwood for his wonderful photographs. Waring
very kindly provided their legendary blender and their muscular juicing
machine for testing and shooting. Thanks also to Michael van Straten,
my friend and former colleague from LBC Newstalk Radio in London,
who is always so sensible about nutrition and complementary medicine.
My brother-in-law, Ron Bray of Kallangur, Queensland, Australia, provided
ongoing advice on the nutritional content and farming peculiarities of all
manner of fruits and vegetables. Friend and colleague Maddie Bastianelli
helped with research.

First published in Great Britain in 2000
This paperback edition published in 2005
by Ryland Peters & Small
20–21 Jockey's Fields, London WC1R 4BW
www.rylandpeters.com

10 9 8 7 6 5 4 3 2 1

Text © Elsa Petersen-Schepelern 2000
Design and photographs © Ryland Peters & Small 2000

Printed and bound in China

ISBN 1 84172 833 0

A CIP record for this book is available from the British Library.

## Notes

All spoon measurements are level unless
otherwise stated.

All fruits and vegetables used in this book
should be washed thoroughly and peeled in the
usual way, unless otherwise advised. Carrots in
particular should be peeled, topped and tailed,
and apples and pears should be cored before
juicing. Unwaxed citrus fruits and cucumbers
should be used whenever possible.

# contents

# introduction

Medical authorities maintain that we should have at least five servings of fruit and vegetables per day. I don't know about you, but three or four is as many as I normally manage. What better way to increase your uptake of healthful foods than to have them in juice form.

**Which juicer?** There are many kinds of juicer on the market, from the humble lemon squeezer (hard to improve on, really) to state-of-the-art extractors. Which should you choose? It depends on your budget, and perhaps even the size of your family or if you're a vegetarian. My own view is that you should get the best and strongest you can afford, and large enough so that you're not tempted to put it away in a cupboard and forget about it. Big is beautiful, and it will stay out on the kitchen bench. Mine has two separate mechanisms – one for citrus and one for everything else.

**How long can you keep juice?** No time at all. If you squeeze fresh orange juice and put it in a jug, it will start to separate in a matter of moments. The whole point of freshly squeezed juice is to drink it straight away. So do. Oxidization starts to happen within minutes, depending on the kind of juice. Think of an apple and how quickly that turns brown. It's still edible, but it's better for you and tastes better if you juice it and drink it immediately. That way, all the antioxidants in the juice will busily mop up any excess free radicals in the body – those 'baddies' that cause cell damage.

**How many ingredients?** I think the fewer the better. If you add too many flavours, they all start to meld together and taste a little like fruity mud. Some juices however, like beetroot and spinach, are good for you in small quantities, but not so good (and not so nice) in large dollops. So mix the small doses of goodies with 'extenders' like apple or orange juice.

**Sweet and salt?** There's no denying, fruits these days don't often get a chance to ripen on the tree, so are distinctly sour. You can always add sugar of course (or honey, which is really just sugar) but the best way in my opinion is to add apple juice, nature's sweetener. And some vegetable juices really do need a pinch of salt to point up their flavours. But if you don't approve of salt, add a squeeze of lemon juice, which will do much the same thing.

In the case of fruits and vegetables that discolour quickly, add a squeeze of citrus juice to slow down the process.

So, to increase your vitamin intake, juicing is the thing. You can always freeze the leftover juices and use them to chill drinks, or churn them into sorbets or cook them in soups – which, incidentally, is an excellent use for the pulp left over after juicing, as is baking.

**Tonics from herbs and spices** Herbs and spices are age-old ways to flavour food and to gently influence the body. Rosemary tea will wake you up: lavender tea will help you nod off. Ordinary tea (which is, after all, just another kind of herb) will spark you up. Cardamom and ginger will calm an upset stomach: star anise and lemon are simply comforting. All are delicious ways to increase your liquid intake (and NONE of us gets enough of that!)

# fruits

**Health Note:** Apples are an important source of Vitamin C and are used to combat fluid retention and constipation. They are particularly good for the heart and vascular system and can help to lower cholesterol levels. **Mint** helps digestion and **ginger** will calm an upset stomach.

apple

# Minty Ginger Granny Smith

Any apples will do, but unpeeled Granny Smiths produce
the most beautiful green. The ginger is optional, but utterly
delicious, and the mint leaves give an even brighter green.
Just a hint – we professional dieters know to use apple
juice instead of sugar to add sweetness. Lime juice will stop
the apple juice turning brown so quickly, but drink this
concoction immediately – don't let it hang around, or you
lose all the benefits of freshly crushed juice.

**4 Granny Smiths, cored but not peeled, then cut into chunks**
**a chunk of fresh ginger, peeled and sliced**
**4–8 sprigs of mint**
**1 tablespoon fresh lime juice (optional)**
**Serves 1**

Push half the apples through the tube, then the ginger, mint and lime
juice, if using, then the remaining apples.

Variation: Frozen Apple Margarita
Put 250 ml crushed ice into a blender, add the juice and blend to a
froth. The Margarita is ready when the sound of the motor changes –
that means the mixture has risen away from the blades.

# Pomegranate Squeeze

Pomegranates have an intriguing sweet-tart flavour and a colour straight out of the Arabian Nights. In the Middle East and Pakistan, the fruit are the size of grapefruit, a deep purple-red, with juice to match.

**3 pomegranates**
**1 orange (optional)**
**1 tablespoon grenadine (optional)**
**Serves 1**

Cut the pomegranates in half around the middle. Using a lemon squeezer, squeeze the juice from the pomegranates and orange. Add grenadine, if using, then serve over ice.

# pomegranate

**Health Note:**   Pomegranates are very low in calories, but rich in phosphorus - important for building good bones and absorbing nutrients. Their sweet-tart flavour is very refreshing in hot weather. Mix them with orange juice for a slightly sweeter drink, and don't press the seeds too hard, or bitter flavours will be released.

**Health Note:** Like apples, **pears** are a gentle digestive and helpful in lowering cholesterol. They are high in potassium, which regulates blood pressure, and in Vitamins C, B1 and B2. In combination with **ginger**, they help calm the digestion as well as tasting wonderful.

**pears**

# Gingered Pear Juice

Commercially produced pear juice is delicious – but when freshly squeezed, especially over ice, it's out of this world. There also seems to be a particular affinity between pears and ginger. Pears must be eaten on the day they become ripe – left longer, their texture becomes 'sleepy'. Juicing is their saviour.

**2–3 pears, quartered and cored**
**a chunk of fresh ginger, peeled**
**and sliced**
**Serves 1**

Juice 1 pear, then the ginger, then the remaining pear or pears. Serve immediately.

# pineapple

**Health Note:** Fresh **pineapple** contains the enzyme bromelian, which helps with digestion. In fact it makes short work of fats and proteins, so is very good for dieters. It is soothing for sore throats, coughs and upset stomachs.

**1 large pineapple**
**1 lemon**
**ice cubes**
**4 passionfruit (optional)**
**sugar or honey, to taste**
**Serves 4**

Put the pineapple through the juicer, add the juice of 1 lemon and pour into a jug of ice. Stir in the flesh and seeds of 3 passionfruit and top with the remainder. Depending on the sweetness and ripeness of the pineapple, you may like to add a little sugar or honey.

# Pineapple Crush

**Health Note:** All fruits contain Vitamin C, but oranges remain the benchmark against which all others are measured. Vitamin C is vital for life and fresh fruit and juice is the best way of getting it. Commercial juices are often pasteurized or heat-treated to sterilize and preserve them. Heat destroys Vitamin C, so manufacturers replace it in the form of Ascorbic Acid. Remember, real fruit contains real vitamins.

orange

# Apricot, Berry and Orange

Apricots are very dense, so you may like to pulp them in the blender rather than putting them through the juicer. If you do decide to juice, remove the skins first*, and juice them alternately with pieces of apple.

**8 ripe apricots, halved and pitted, then coarsely chopped**
**8 strawberries, hulled and halved**
**juice of 2 oranges**
**Serves 1**

Put the apricots, strawberries and orange juice in a blender. Whizz until smooth, adding water if needed. (If the mixture is too thick, add a few ice cubes and whizz again.)

*To remove the skins, bring a saucepan of water to the boil, then blanch the apricots for about 1 minute. Remove and pull off the skin with the back of a knife.

# Blueberries and Orange

**4 oranges**
**1 punnet blueberries (250 g)**
**Serves 1–2**

Squeeze the oranges, then put the juice in a blender with the berries and whizz until smooth. Alternatively, I often peel the oranges, then chop them up and feed half of them through a juicer, followed by the blueberries, then the remaining oranges.

# Strawberries and Balsamic

Balsamic, the rich, slightly sweet, aged vinegar from Italy, should be used in moderation – use it like a spice, don't slap it on like ordinary vinegar. It also has an extraordinary affinity with strawberries. Rinse the berries before hulling, or they will fill with water.

**2 punnets ripe strawberries**
**1 tablespoon honey (optional)**
**To serve:**
**balsamic vinegar**
**ice cubes**
**Serves 2–4**

Reserve a few strawberries for decoration, then put the remainder in a blender with the honey, if using, and a cupful of ice cubes. Zap, adding water if necessary to make the mixture easier to blend. Zap again, then serve over ice, with a halved strawberry on top. Serve the balsamic separately, in drops.

# strawberries

Health Note: Strawberries, like many other berries, help protect against cancer. The juice can also be used in small quantities combined with other juices, or to flavour yoghurt drinks. **Vinegar** is an aid to digestion, prevents fatigue and lessens the risk of high blood pressure.

# melon

**Health Note:** Melons are
perfect for dieters,
being mostly water, and
make delicious juices.
They move quickly and
gently through the
system, and are best
eaten at the beginning
of a meal rather than
the end.

# Melon Froth

These four melon varieties are my favourites – all very aromatic. My juicer produces a froth, but if yours is less muscular, you could layer the juices to form orange and green stripes. Wonderful for a summer lunch party.

**1–2 melons – orange cantaloupe or charentais, or green**
**    galia or honeydew, halved, deseeded and peeled**
**ginger syrup, to taste (optional)**
**Serves 1–2**

Put the melons through a juicer. Layer the colours in glasses if preferred, or serve separately. Serve ginger syrup separately, if using.

# Watermelon and Lime Slush

**red flesh from 1 round watermelon**
**a chunk of fresh ginger, grated**
**To serve:**
**2 limes, cut into wedges**
**crushed ice**
**Serves 4**

Press the melon flesh and ginger through a
juicer, then pour into a jug half full of
crushed ice. Serve immediately in glasses with
lime wedges or use to make sorbet.
If serving as a sorbet, add sugar to taste (the
mixture should be very sweet), then churn in
an ice cream machine. Alternatively, part-
freeze in metal trays, then zap in a food
processor and freeze again. Just before
serving, crush into an icy slush.

# watermelon

**Health Note:**  Watermelons are mostly water, so they are refreshing and very good for dieters. The succulent flesh is high in Vitamin C. **Limes,** also high in Vitamin C, are good for pointing up the flavour, preserving the colour and slowing down the oxidization process. But don't wait around - juice and drink as soon as possible. Alternatively, churn and freeze, then serve as a slush.

# Mexican Golden Salsa Crush

These three vegetables originally came from Mexico. I am not very fond of fiery-hot chillies, so one medium-hot one is perfect for me. Add more if you like, or use a hotter one. The pinch of salt is optional, but salt points up the flavours beautifully. You could use a dash of lemon juice instead. The real, raw juice is sweet enough for me.

**1–2 red, orange or yellow peppers, halved and deseeded**
**1 medium-hot red chilli, deseeded**
**2 tomatoes, quartered**
**a pinch of salt (optional) or a squeeze of lemon juice**
**Serves 1**

Feed half the peppers into the juicer, then the chile, tomato, remaining peppers and a pinch of salt, if using, or lemon juice.

# vegetables

**Health note:** **Peppers** and their hot-headed **chilli** cousins have three times as much Vitamin C as an orange. Juicing removes the indigestible skins and extracts all the sweet flavour.

pepper

Health Note:  Beetroot, famous as a blood tonic, is a powerhouse of vitamins and minerals - A, B group and C, plus calcium, iron and potassium. Beetroot is good for blood pressure, protects against anaemia and promotes general good health.

beetroot

# Beetroot and Orange

Raw beetroot is good for you, but only in small quantities – and it has a decidedly earthy taste. Trimming and peeling before juicing will help, but best of all is 'stretching' it with freshly squeezed juice such as orange or even apple. Depending on the sweetness of the oranges, you may need a little honey stirred through the juice.

**1 medium beetroot, trimmed and**
**  peeled if preferred**
**2–3 oranges**
**honey, to taste**
**Serves 1**

Cut the beetroot into pieces and press through a juice extractor. Squeeze the oranges. Mix together, stir and taste, adding honey if necessary.

**Note:** Beetroot leaves are also delicious. Either juice them separately or with spinach leaves – or sauté in a little olive oil and serve as an accompaniment to main courses.

# fennel

**Health Note:** Like celery, fennel bulbs are low in calories and traditionally have been used to combat indigestion. **Fennel** contains beta carotene and folate, an important ingredient for pregnant women. **Apples** help maintain a healthy immune system.

Fennel can be very difficult to juice – you need a strong machine. Alternatively, chop it and purée in a blender with apple juice, then strain. Use a crisp, sweet apple such as Red Delicious to give a wonderful pinkish tinge. Always remember to remove the stem and stalk ends of apples and pears, where any pesticides and residues collect.

**1 fennel bulb, including sprigs of the feathery leaves**
**2 apples, cored but not peeled**
**juice of ½ lemon (optional)**
**Serves 1–2**

Trim the green leaves from the fennel bulb, trim off the root end, then slice the bulb into long wedges and cut out and remove the cores from each wedge. Cut the apple into wedges. Put both through a juicer.
Stir in the lemon juice to stop discoloration, then serve immediately, topped with a few fennel sprigs for extra scent.

# Fennel and Apple

# Celery and Grapes

Celery juice is marvellous when mixed with other vegetable juices – but also with juicy fruits such as grapes. You can buy grape juice, but fresh juice is a revelation. White grapes will produce a fresh green juice – red or black ones a delicious pink-tinged nectar.

**6 celery stalks, trimmed**
**about 20 seedless white grapes**
**1 bunch watercress (optional)**
**ice cubes**
**Serves 1–2**

Push the celery stalks into the juicer, leaf end first. Alternate with the grapes, which are very soft and difficult to push through on their own. Press through the watercress, if using, and serve plain, in glasses filled with ice, or zapped with ice cubes in a blender to produce a delicious celery-grape froth.

**Health Note:** Celery has almost no calories - it's like eating water, so is marvellous for dieters. All fruits and vegetables contain phytochemicals which help the body fight disease - but celery is especially good for people who have gout, rheumatism or high blood pressure. Celery is a natural tranquilizer and helps relieve fluid retention. Celery and grapes help protect against arthritis and gout, and alleviate joint pains. (Grapes are always good mixed with other juices.)

celery

# Lettuce and Parsley Crush

Lettuce and parsley produce small quantities of juice and taste decidedly green! So add the juice of an apple or other fruit as an extender and sweetener. As many good cooks know, much of the flavour in parsley is in the stalks, so juice them too. Before juicing, all leafy vegetables should be washed well, wrapped in a cloth and refrigerated until crisp.

**1 cos or iceberg lettuce, stalk trimmed**
**1 large bunch of parsley, including stalks, ends trimmed**
**1 green apple, cored but not peeled**
**Serves 1**

Form the lettuce and parsley leaves into balls and push through the juicer feed tube. Lastly, to extract more juice, press an apple through. Stir if necessary, then serve immediately – don't wait.

# parsley

**Health Note:** **Parsley** is famous as a breath freshener and an effective digestive. **Lettuce** is high in antioxidants, which prevent infection and protect against some cancers, heart disease and premature aging. Both ingredients discolour quickly after being cut, so juice them and drink immediately. Dark-green leafy vegetables contain beneficial folic acid and bioflavonoids, so use the greenest variety of lettuce you can, such as cos or romaine. The iceberg is a particularly juicy variety. Make an infusion of parsley as a hair rinse to make your hair shiny.

# cucumber

Health Note: **Cucumber** is low in calories but rich in Vitamins B1, B2 and C and minerals calcium and iron. It is a natural diuretic. Raw spinach, though good for you, should not be taken in very large doses. It contains oxalic acid which locks up other vitamins so they can't be used by the body. In spite of its Popeye reputation, spinach isn't particularly high in iron. When it was retested in the 1940s, it was found that someone had put the decimal point in the wrong place!

# Cucumber and Spinach

Yes, spinach is good for you – but too much isn't. Spinach juice is also no-one's idea of a good time, but mix it with something more delicious and you'll absorb all its goodness almost painlessly. Take care – cucumbers are often waxed, but organically grown produce won't be. If you can find only the waxed kind, you'll have to peel them and so lose most of the colour and many of the nutrients.

**1 organic cucumber, about 30 cm long, quartered lengthways**
**1 large handful well-washed spinach**
**salt or lemon juice, to taste (optional)**
**Serves 1–2**

Juice half the cucumber, then all the spinach, then the remaining cucumber. Add salt or lemon juice to taste, if using.

Variation:
Cucumber has a cooling, astringent effect – to sweeten it, use half-and-half with apple juice from crisp Granny Smiths.

# carrot

**Health Note:** Carrots are high in beta carotene, which the body uses to convert into Vitamin A. The nutrients are easier to digest when cooked, but carrot juice is utterly delicious. Don't have this drink more than twice a week, or you run the risk of developing an orange tinge to your skin!

# Carrot and Ginger Crush

Carrot juice, so naturally sweet, is my absolutely favourite juice. Though carrots are better for you when cooked, I much prefer them raw. Just make sure you peel them first, unless they have been organically grown.

**5 medium carrots, peeled**
**a chunk of fresh ginger, peeled and**
**sliced (optional)**
**Serves 1–2**

Cut the carrots into pieces small enough to fit through the feeder tube. When half the carrots have been processed, add the ginger, if using, then the rest of the carrots.

# Fresh Virgin Mary

Make Bloody Mary with fresh juices and your friends will love you forever. Fresh tomato juice is thinner and sweeter than the commercial kinds – and more delicious.

**6 ripe tomatoes**
**3 celery stalks**
**1 garlic clove (optional)**
**1 red chilli, deseeded**
**ice cubes**
**a dash of Worcestershire sauce (optional)**
**Serves 1**

To skin the tomatoes, cut a small cross in the base, put into a large bowl and cover with boiling water. Leave for 1 minute, then drain and pull off the skins. Juice the tomatoes, celery, garlic, if using, and chilli. Pour into a jug of ice, stir in the Worcestershire sauce, if using, then serve (with or without vodka).

Variations: Add other fruit and vegetable juices such as broccoli, cabbage, lemon or radish – and a dash of Moroccan harissa paste.

**Health Note:** The tomato is probably the world's single most wonderful vegetable (though it's technically a fruit). Tomatoes are low in calories but high in Vitamins C and E, plus potassium, beta carotene and lycopene, which helps some forms of cancer by preventing damage by free radicals. **Garlic** is one of nature's medicines, lowering cholesterol and blood pressure, protecting against cancer, soothing coughs and colds and aiding digestion. It also contains polyphenols, which protect the heart.

French tisanes are infusions of herbs, flowers or leaves, usually dried. I prefer them made with fresh ingredients where possible. In early times, they were seen as cures for many ailments. Nowadays, people drink them because they taste good. A *tisanière* is a tall, lidded cup, with a strainer inside to hold the herb. If you don't have one (they are to be found in antique shops), use a cafetière (coffee press) instead.

**4–6 sprigs of rosemary**
**1–2 teaspoons honey**
**Serves 1–2**

Put the rosemary and honey in a cafetière or teapot, cover with boiling water, let infuse for about 5 minutes, then plunge or strain.

Variations: Tisanes are also made with camomile flowers, lemon balm, marjoram, sage, thyme and orange blossoms.

# Rosemary Tisane

# teas and tisanes

**Health Note:
Rosemary** tea will
wake you up, so
drink it only in
the morning (it's
also good for
a hangover).
Do not use while
pregnant or when
breast-feeding.

## rosemary

**Health Note:** Cardamom **and ginger** help with indigestion, nausea, coughs and colds. Brew them, separately or together, in tea or coffee, with or without milk. Tea, especially **green tea,** is high in bioflavonoids - antioxidants, which help protect against heart disease and cancer.

# cardamom

# Cardamom Green Tea

An idea from Pakistan, which makes
the world's most wonderful tea: a pot
of green tea contains an aromatic
treasure – a spoonful of green
cardamom pods. Cardamom and
ginger are both powerful soothing
agents for upset stomachs.

**1 teaspoon green tea, plus 1 for
the pot**
**6 green cardamom pods**
**sugar, to taste**
**Serves 2**

Rinse the teapot with boiling water, add the
tea and cardamom, then fill with boiling
water. Let steep for 1–2 minutes only (no
longer, or the bitter tannins are released).
Pour the tea and add sugar only if you
usually like sweet tea.

**1 large bunch of mint**
**sugar or honey, to taste (optional)**
**1 tablespoon green tea (optional)**
**Serves 1–4**

Wash the mint well, then break it in large handfuls and put into a cafetière.
Pour over boiling water, let steep for 3–5 minutes, then press the plunger. Pour into tea
glasses, add honey, if using, and a few fresh mint leaves, then serve. If using green tea, add it
at the same time as the mint.

# Mint Tea

**Health Note:** Mint is a stimulant, so don't drink it late at night. It will help digestion and relieve an upset stomach. Do not use while pregnant or when breast-feeding.

mint

# Lavender Tea

The very essence of a hot summer
afternoon in Italy or the South of
France, lavender tea is very calming –
good to drink before bed.

**1–2 branches lavender leaves**
**a few lavender flowers, if available**
**1 teaspoon honey, or to taste**
**Serves 1**

Put the lavender in a teapot or one-cup
cafetière and and cover with boiling water.
Let steep for 5 minutes, covered.
Put 1 teaspoon honey, if using, in your cup,
then press the plunger and pour the tea.
Alternatively, pour the honey over the
lavender in the cafetière before adding the
boiling water.

# lavender

**Health Note:**
Lavender is a decongestant, general tonic and immunity booster. It is mildly sedative, so good to drink before bed or when you need to relax. It is also very soothing for people prone to overwork.

**Health Note:**
Lemons and limes are high in Vitamin C and become sweeter and juicier as they ripen. They have an antibacterial and decongestant action, so are excellent for coughs and colds. The juice is good for the digestion and for people who suffer from joint pain. The sharp taste of lemon can can be used instead of salt to enhance other flavours.

# lemons and limes

**1 litre freshly made tea, lightly brewed**
**sugar, to taste**
**1–2 unwaxed limes, finely sliced**
**ice cubes**
**mineral water, lemonade or ginger ale**
**Serves 4**

Strain the tea, stir in the sugar, cool and chill.
Put sliced limes in a jug, then half-fill it with
ice cubes. Half-fill the jug with the cold tea,
then top up with mineral water, lemonade
or ginger ale, stir and serve.

# Iced Lime Tea

**1 unwaxed lemon**
**1 pot of tea**
**1 tablespoon honey**
**Serves 1**

Cut 2 slices off the lemon and squeeze the
juice from the rest. Put the honey and sliced
lemon in a large mug, add the lemon juice,
then top with tea. Stir and drink.

# Hot Lemon Tea with Honey

If you like aniseed flavours, like liquorice or pastis, you'll love this drink. Tea is always best made with leaves, but this recipe can also be made with your favourite brand of tea bag. I like it not too strong and served without milk.

**1 tea bag, such as English Breakfast**
**1 whole star anise**
**sweetener, to taste**
**milk (optional)**
**Serves 1**

Put the tea bag and star anise in a cup, add sweetener if you usually use it, then pour over boiling water. Add milk if preferred. Let steep for your usual amount of time, then remove the tea bag and serve.

## Star Anise Tea

**Health Note:** Star anise is
a delicious breath freshener.
It also stimulates the appetite
and calms a growling tummy. It
can act both as a stimulant and
as a sedative. Tea, especially green
tea, is high in antioxidants, which
help the body protect itself against
heart disease and cancer.

# star anise

# ginger

**Health Note:** Ginger is an all-purpose tonic. It is astonishing in its ability to calm an upset stomach, but it can also help with the pain of arthritis and indigestion. It will also soothe coughs and colds.

# Ginger Tea

**a chunk of fresh ginger**
**1 teaspoon leaf tea (optional)**
**sweetener of your choice**
**Serves 1**

Peel and grate the ginger. (The cheese-grater shown here is quick, clean and easy.) Put in a tea strainer or tea ball set in the cup, then add the tea, if using. Add boiling water and let steep for 1–5 minutes, according to how strong you like the flavour. Add sweetener if you like, then sip slowly. The same ginger can be used for extra cups.

# Almond Milk

Nut milks are delicious for people who 'don't do dairy'. You can make them with any nuts, but almonds are easy to find. You can use unblanched almonds (with their skins still on), but the result is browner and grittier. To blanch your own almonds, put in a bowl, cover with boiling water, leave for 5 minutes, then pop them out of their skins.

**1 packet almonds, preferably blanched (about 100 g)**
**1 tablespoon honey**
**250 ml ice cubes or crushed ice**
**Serves 1**

Put the almonds and honey in a blender, add the ice cubes and 250 ml ice water. Zap to a paste. Gradually add extra iced water until the mixture is smooth. Strain and serve over ice.

**Note:** The process can be repeated several times, producing thinner and thinner 'milk' each time. Eventually, the strained almond meal can be used to thicken sauces or flavour breads, cakes or biscuits.

# nut milks and yoghurt

nuts

**Health Note:** Almond milk is a classic invalid food, a true tonic. All nuts are high in protein (important for vegetarians) and in oils. They also contain Vitamin E - a powerful antioxidant - which is more beneficial in foods, rather than in pill form. Almonds also contain minerals such as zinc, magnesium, potassium, calcium and iron.

# mango

**Health Note:** Eating ripe fresh **mangoes** is good for the skin and for people with high blood pressure. Mangoes are better blended rather than juiced and are good mixed with other ingredients, such as coconut milk or yoghurt. Take care when peeling them, and don't eat the flesh straight from the skin, because sap from the stem and peel can cause blisters. (When a mango is properly ripe, you should be able to pull the skin off the fruit as shown. If you have to use a knife, it's not ripe.)

# Mango and Coconut Milk

Another nut-milk recipe, particularly good for people who are lactose-intolerant – and for anyone lucky enough to have too many mangoes.

**2 fresh ripe mangoes, peeled and
   pitted, or 250 ml mango purée
juice of ½ lime or lemon
250 ml desiccated coconut (measured
   by volume), or canned coconut milk
Serves 2**

Blend the mangoes with the lime or lemon juice, then transfer to a jug and chill.
If using desiccated coconut, put it in a blender with 250 ml iced water. Blend until frothy, let stand for 5 minutes, then blend again. Strain into the jug and return the coconut to the blender. Repeat with another 250 ml iced water. Strain, then stir into the jug of mango and lime or lemon. Serve immediately. Alternatively, omit the coconut milk and just blend the mango and lime or lemon juice with enough ice cubes and water to make a pourable consistency.

# Fruit Ice Blocks with Buttermilk Froth

Freeze a selection of fresh juices in an ice cube tray and serve with buttermilk for a delicious breakfast on a hot day.

**1 tray ice cubes made of fruit juices**
**100 ml buttermilk or low-fat yoghurt**
**sparkling mineral water or soda water**
**Serves 4**

Fill 4 glasses with the fruity ice cubes, add a dollop of buttermilk or yoghurt, then top with sparkling mineral water or soda water. The ice cubes melt slowly into the drink, so you can top it up with more buttermilk or more mineral water for a long, cool, delicious and filling drink.

# buttermilk

**Health Note:** Traditionally, **buttermilk** was the part of the milk left when all the fats (butters) had been churned away. Modern buttermilks are simply skimmed milks with a light culture, similar to yoghurt, added. Mix it with icy fruit squeezes - ice cubes made from fruit juice melt more slowly than ordinary cubes - so they're good for a long, leisurely breakfast.

As with most milk products, buttermilk is high in calcium. It is also low in fat, while the bio-culture is good for the digestion.

# banana

Health Note:  Bananas are high in complex carbohydrates — that's why tennis players eat them at Wimbledon. Very nourishing and good for the cholesterol levels, they are energy foods, rich in potassium, Vitamins A, C and K. A meal in themselves, they are wonderful for breakfast and very good for growing children.

# Papaya and Banana Smoothie

Papayas and bananas won't juice effectively – their pulp is too dense – but are definitely candidates for the blender treatment. If your blender doesn't crush ice, add it at the end, but, to help the machine run, you will need a little water, yoghurt or juice.

**1 small papaya, peeled, deseeded and cut into chunks**
**1 banana, peeled and cut into chunks**
**250 ml ice**
**125 ml yoghurt (optional)**
**1 tablespoon wheatgerm (optional)**
**Serves 2–4**

Put the papaya and banana into a blender with the ice and 125 ml water or yoghurt, if using. Pulse until smooth, then add the wheatgerm, if using, and extra water or yoghurt to form a pourable consistency.

Variation:
Blueberries and banana make a famous combination. Blend them with ice, yoghurt and a dash of honey, if preferred.

# Red Berry Smoothie

Even people with dairy intolerance are often able to eat yoghurt, since it changes its structure during fermentation. It's marvellous for people with upset stomachs too!

**1 punnet berries (about 250 g),
such as strawberries, cranberries, red
currants or raspberries (for a pink
smoothie) or blackberries and
blueberries (for a blue smoothie)**
**250 ml plain yoghurt**
**125 ml crushed ice**
**Serves 2–3**

Put all the ingredients in a blender and work to a thin, frothy cream. If too thick, add water to create a pourable consistency.

# berries

**Health Note:** **Berries** are high in vitamin C and antioxidants which protect against cancer and heart disease and help ease the pain of arthritis. A daily helping of 1 cup blueberries contains enough antioxidants to improve balance, coordination, and short-term memory. Strawberries also improve memory. Most berries are better blended rather than juiced, and are good mixed with other fruits or with yogurt in smoothies and lassis.

Plain low-fat yogurt is the best form of calcium for women and is helpful in treating digestive disorders.

# index